D0208050

Contents

Introduction

Singing is fun, and learning to sing and lead songs is an important part of your patrol and troop program.

Songs are a natural for troop meetings, hikes, camping trips, or when you and your buddies are simply working together.

A good songfest is a part of most campfire programs. Around a blazing campfire you and your fellow Scouts will enjoy singing most.

Songs will create enthusiasm and set a mood for your meetings.

The songs in this book are the kind Scouts are singing every day at camp, troop meetings, and on hikes. Ranging from songs for gay moments to those for quieter times, they are the favorites of Scouts and Scouters across America.

Song Leading

Relax, you don't have to be a professional singer or the director of a symphony to lead campfire songs. Use simple deliberate up-and-down motions with one or both hands to fit the beat or the words. With practice you can develop a style of your own.

For the first song you lead, choose one that is simple and well known by the group. Try an old favorite as a warmer-upper.

Select your songs in advance and be sure you know them well enough to teach them with ease.

Set the pitch for songs by humming or singing the first few bars.

Get the correct pitch and the whole group will sing easily. If you pitch your song too high or too low, stop the song, get the correct pitch, and start over.

Loud singing in good spirit is fine, but a group shouting a song to make noise will soon get out of control.

Never ask the group what song they would like to sing. You will receive too many suggestions and become confused. Be enthusiastic and wear a smile as you lead songs. The way you feel will soon catch on with the group you are leading.

To teach a song, sing it through a couple of times so the boys have a chance to learn the words and tune. Then try quietly singing it together, so everyone will get the feel of it.

An instrumental background will help, even if it is provided by only a single instrument such as a harmonica or guitar. Guitar chords are shown for each song.

Try to organize a singing group in your troop. This group will make a nucleus for a good song session. It can learn new songs in advance and put them across when taught to the troop.

At campfires, follow the fire as you lead songs. Begin with lively songs while the flames leap high. As the fire dies down, sing quiet songs. Close meetings, campfires, or songfests with songs that have a patriotic or inspirational flavor. Lasting impressions will be made as boys quietly sing a favorite closing song.

Songs of Greeting

Hail, Hail, the Gang's All Here

Hail! Hail!— the gang's all here,— Nev-er mind the weath-er Here we are to-geth-er. Hail! Hail!— the gang's all here,— Let the fun be-gin right now.— now.—

How Do You Do?

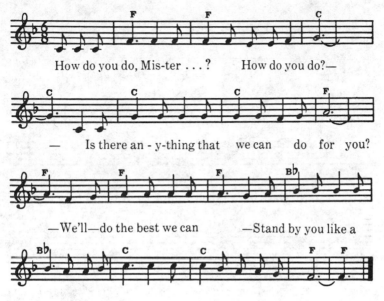

How do you do, Mis-ter . . . ? How do you do?—

— Is there an - y-thing that we can do for you?

—We'll—do the best we can —Stand by you like a

man. How do you do Mis-ter . . . ? How do you do?

Substitute name of person being honored in place of dotted lines.

Hello! Hello!

Key: E Flat.   Time: 4/4

Divide the singers into four groups; each sings one Hello *and holds it through to the completion of the full chord. Sing the middle part in unison.*

Hel - lo, Hel - lo,   Hel - lo,   We're glad to meet you,

We're glad to greet you. Hel - lo, hel - lo, hel - lo, hel - lo.

We're Here for Fun

Tune: "Auld Lang Syne"

We're here for fun right from the start,
  So drop your dignity!
Just laugh and sing with all your heart,
  And show your loyalty.
May all your troubles be forgot,
  Let this night be the best;
Join in the songs we sing tonight,
  Be happy with the rest.

We're All Together Again, We're Here

We're all to-geth-er a-gain, we're here, we're here.— We're all to-geth-er a-gain, we're here, we're here.— And who knows when we'll be all to-geth-er a-gain? sing-ing

All to-geth-er a-gain, we're here.—

O Dad O' Mine

Tune: "Sweet Adeline"   Key: B Flat.   Time: 4/4
   Boys use Dad. *Fathers echo with* Lad.

O Dad o' mine (O Lad o' mine),
Dear Dad o' mine (Dear Lad o' mine),
We'll stand as one (We'll stand as one),
In rain or shine (In rain or shine);
Each night and day (Each night and day),
I'll always say (I'll always say),
You're the best friend in the world,
O Dad o' mine (O Lad o' mine).

Copyrighted title used by permission of M. Witmark and Sons, N.Y.

The More We Get Together

Tune: "Ach Du Lieber Augustine"   Key of F

The more we get together, together, together,
The more we get together, the happier we'll be.
For your friends are my friends,
And my friends are your friends,
The more we get together, the happier we'll be.

The more we get together, together, together,
The more we get together, the happier we'll be.
For you know that I know,
And I know that you know,
The more we get together, the happier we'll be.

Action Songs

Three Wood Pigeons

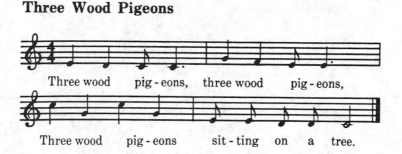

Three wood pig-eons, three wood pig-eons,

Three wood pig-eons sit-ting on a tree.

Leader: Look! One has flown away?
Group: Oh! *Wailing*

Two wood pigeons, two wood pigeons, etc.
Leader: Look! Another has flown!
Group: Oh-h-h! *Louder wailing*

One wood pigeon, one wood pigeon, etc.
Leader: Oh, oh, oh! There goes the last one!
Group: Oh-h-h! *Very loud wailing*

No wood pigeons, no wood pigeons, etc.
Leader: Look! One has returned! *Joyfully*
Group: Ah-h!

One wood pigeon, etc.
Leader: Another has returned! *Loud cheers*
Two wood pigeons, etc. *More rapidly*

Leader: Hurray! The third one has returned! *Tremendous cheers*
Three wood pigeons, etc. *Rapidly and enthusiastically*

Variation: Three persons may represent the pigeons and "fly" in or out with comical antics.

John Brown's Baby

Tune: "John Brown's Body"

John Brown's baby had a cold upon its chest,
John Brown's baby had a cold upon its chest,
John Brown's baby had a cold upon its chest,
And they rubbed it up with camphorated oil,.

Motions

1st time—sing straight through

2d time—omit singing "baby" and substitute motion of rocking baby

3d time—omit "cold" and substitute a coughing sound

4th time—same as third only substitute striking chest for "chest"

5th time—same as fourth only omit last line and rub chest

The Grand Old Duke of York

Tune: "A-Hunting We Will Go"

The grand old Duke of York,
He had ten thousand men.
He marched them up the hill,
Everyone stands up
And marched them down again.
Everyone sits down
And when you're up, you're up;
Everyone up
And when you're down, you're down.
Everyone down
And When you're only halfway up,
Everyone halfway up
You're niether up nor down.
All up   All down

Repeat several times; each time getting faster.

Ravioli

Tune: "Alouette"

All: Ravioli, I like ravioli.
   Ravioli, it's the best for me.

Leader: Have I got it on my chin?

All: Yes, you got it on your chin.

Leader: On my chin?

All: On you chin. OH-h-h-h-h
   Ravioli, I like ravioli.
   Ravioli, it's the best for me.

(Continue tie, shirt, pants, shoes, floor, walls. Point to the items as each new word is added by the song leader. It is repeated by the chorus and all preceding verses are sung in reverse order.)

All: Ravioli, I like ravioli.
   Ravioli, it's the best for me.

Leader: Is it all over?

All: Yes, it's all over.

Leader: Yes, it's all over.

Bingo

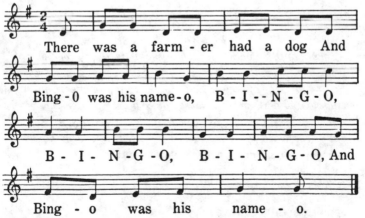

There was a farm-er had a dog And
Bing-o was his name-o, B - I - - N - G - O,
B - I - N - G - O, B - I - N - G - O, And
Bing - o was his name - o.

Sing song through six times, the first time just spelling out the name B-I-N-G-O; second time, spell out first four letters and clap the "O"; third time, spell out first three letters and clap the "G" and "O"; etc., until all five letters are clapped out.

11

I Points to Mineself

I points to mine-self, vas is das here;

Das is mine top-notch-er, ya ma - ma dear.

Top-notch-er, top-notch-er, ya ma- ma dear.

Dat's wot I learned in der school, boom-boom!

As you sing this action-fun song, point to the proper part of your body when you mention it in the song. For example: Point to the top of your head as you sing topnotcher. Continue singing and add another part of your body for each verse and repeat others, going backward from last item to first. Try as many verses as you want, using the list below. For the boom —boom, clap hands, bang on tables, or stamp feet.

Chorus (Repeat after each verse.)

I points to mineself, vas is das here;
Das is mine sweat browser, ya mama dear,
Sweat browser, topnotcher, ya mama dear.
Dat's wot I learned in der school, boom-boom!

Repeat chorus.

Point to	Sing
Top of head	Topnotcher
Brow	Sweat browser
Eye	Eye winker
Nose	Horn blower
Mustache	Soup strainer
Mouth	Lunch eater
Chin	Chin chowser
Neck	Rubber necker
Chest	Chest protector
Tummy	Breadbasket
Foot	Foot stomper

She'll Be Comin' 'Round the Mountain

Novelty arrangement in italics

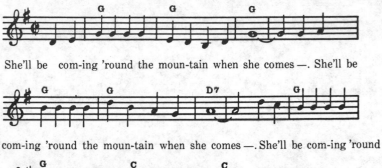

She'll be com-ing 'round the moun-tain when she comes —. She'll be

com-ing 'round the moun-tain when she comes —. She'll be com-ing 'round

the moun-tain, She'll be com-ing 'round the moun-tain, She'll be

com-ing round the moun-tain when she comes.

Sing each stanza and make appropriate gestures three times. Following the last singing of each stanza, repeat sounds and gestures of all preceding stanzas.

For example: At the end of the sixth stanza you say Scratch, scratch!; Yum, yum!; Hack, hack!; Hi, Babe!; Whoa, back!; Woo, hoo! *and go through all the motions.*

She'll be comin' 'round the mountain
When she comes, "Whoo, hoo!"
   Pull down on imaginary whistle cord twice.

She'll be drivin' six white horses
When she comes, "Whoa, back!"
   Pull back on reins.

14

And, we'll all go out to meet her
When she comes, "Hi, Babe!"
  Wave right hand, palm front, left to right.

And we'll kill the old red rooster
When she comes, "Hack, hack!"
  Chopping motion with right hand.

And we'll all have chicken 'n' dumplings
When she comes, "Yum, yum!"
  Rub stomach.

And we'll wear our bright red woollies
When she comes, "Scratch, scratch!"
  Scratch ribs.

Tra, La, La

Swiss

(Refrain) Tra la la la la la   la la la,

Tra la la la la la   la la la,

Tra la la la la la   la la la,

Tra la la la la   la. —

*(Sing the refrain at the beginning and after each verse, swaying
on the refrain and doing the appropriate motions for each verse.)*

1. And in and out, and left and right, etc.
2. And up and down, and left and right, etc.
3. And up and down, and left and right,
   And in and out, and left and right, etc.

If You're Happy

If you're happy and you know it,
Clap your hands. *Clap-clap*
If you're happy and you know it,
Clap your hands. *Clap-clap*
If you're happy and you know it,
Then you really ought to show it,
If you're happy and you know it,
Clap your hands. *Clap-clap*

For following verses, repeat first verse and substitute new words and motions.

If you're happy and you know it,
Stamp your feet. *Stamp-stamp*

16

If you're happy and you know it,
Shout HOORAY!

If you're happy and you know it,
Do all three. *Clap-clap, stamp-stamp,* HOORAY!

One Finger, One Thumb

One fin - ger, one thumb, one hand, Keep
mov - ing. One fin - ger, one thumb, one hand, Keep
mov - ing. One fin - ger, one thumb, one hand, Keep
mov - ing. And we'll all be hap-py and gay.—

2. One finger, one thumb, one hand, two hands,
   Keep moving.
   Repeat three times.
   And we'll all be happy and gay.

Add in turn:
3. One arm
4. Two arms
5. One leg
6. Two legs
7. Stand up—sit down
8. Turn around

NOTE
Words are accompanied by motions with finger, thumb, hand, raising arms, stamping foot, standing-up and sitting-down actions.

Johnnie Verbeck

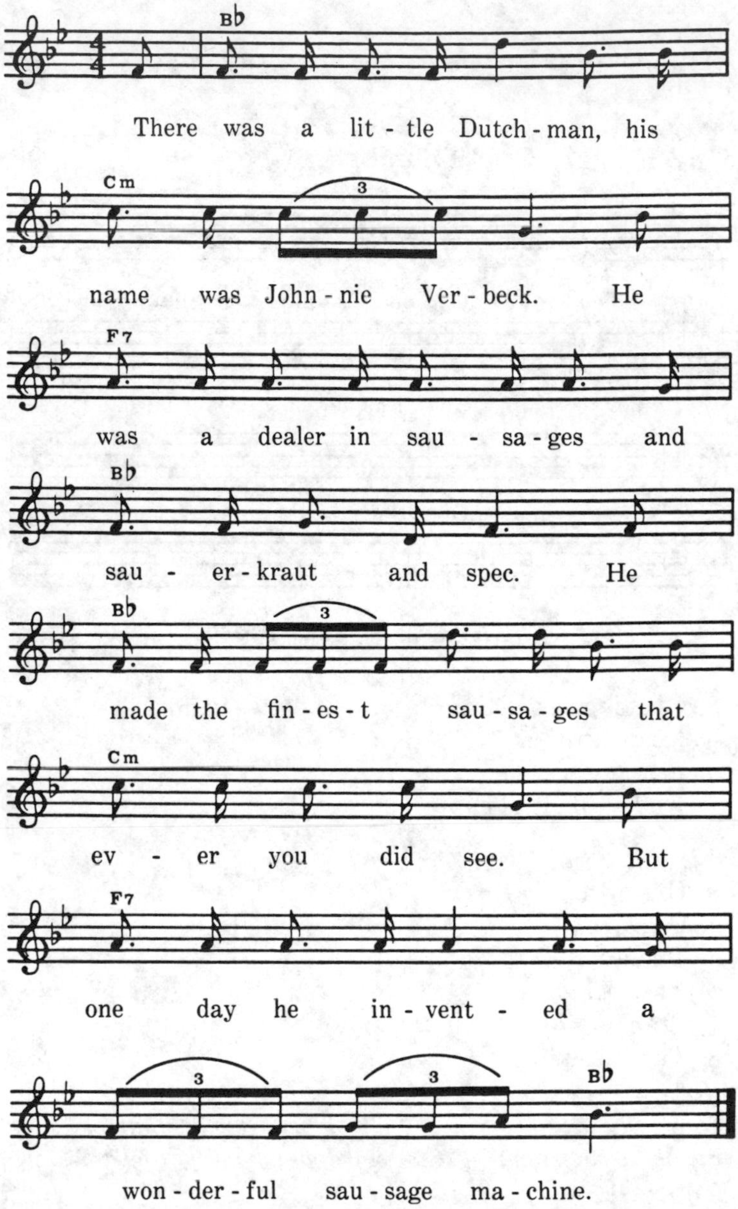

There was a lit - tle Dutch - man, his

name was John - nie Ver - beck. He

was a dealer in sau - sa - ges and

sau - er - kraut and spec. He

made the fin - es - t sau - sa - ges that

ev - er you did see. But

one day he in - vent - ed a

won - der - ful sau - sage ma - chine.

18

Chorus

Oh, Mister Johnnie Verbeck,

How could you be so mean?

I told you you'd be sorry

For inventing that machine.

All the neighbors' cats and dogs

Will never more be seen,

For they'll be ground to sausages

In Johnnie Verbeck's machine.

One day a little fat boy came walking in the store,

He bought a pound of sausage and piled them on the floor;

The boy began to whistle and he whistled up a tune,

And all the little sausages went dancing 'round the room.

Repeat chorus.

One day the machine got busted and the blamed thing
wouldn't go.

So Johnnie Verbeck, he climbed inside to see what made
it so;

His wife, she had a nightmare and walking in her sleep,

She gave the crank an awful yank and Johnnie Verbeck
was meat.

Repeat chorus.

Paw-Paw Patch

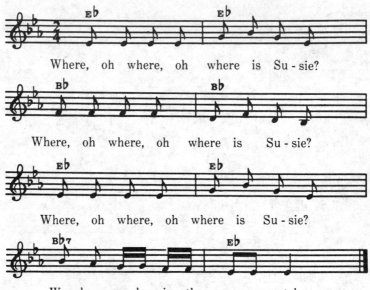

Where, oh where, oh where is Su - sie?

Where, oh where, oh where is Su - sie?

Where, oh where, oh where is Su - sie?

Way down yon-der in the paw-paw patch.

Chorus
Picking up paw-paws; put 'em in a basket.
Picking up paw-paws; put 'em in a basket.
Picking up paw-paws; put 'em in a basket.
Way down yonder in the paw-paw patch.

Come along, boys, and let's go find her.
Come along, boys, and let's go find her.
Come along, boys, and let's go find her.
Way down yonder in the paw-paw patch.

Repeat chorus.

She's a queen of old Hawaii.
She's a queen of old Hawaii.
She's a queen of old Hawaii.
Way down yonder in the paw-paw patch.

Repeat chorus.

She can teach you how to hulu.
She can teach you how to hulu.
She can teach you how to hulu.
Way down yonder in the paw-paw patch.

Repeat chorus.

Pick a Bale of Cotton

Negro work song

Gon - na jump down, turn a - round, Pick a bale of cot-ton, Gon-na

jump down, turn a-round, Pick a bale a day

Oh, Lor-dy, Pick a bale of cot-ton

Oh, Lor-dy. Pick a bale a day.

Me and my wife's gonna pick a bale of cotton,
Me and my wife's gonna pick a bale a day.
Me and my wife's gonna pick a bale of cotton,
Me and my wife's gonna pick a bale a day.

Gonna pick-a, pick-a, pick-a, pick a bale of cotton,
Gonna pick-a, pick-a, pick-a, pick-a, pick a bale a day.
Gonna pick-a, pick-a, pick-a, pick-a, pick a bale of cotton,
Gonna pick-a, pick-a, pick-a, pick-a, pick a bale a day.

Repeat chorus.

Collected and adapted by John A. and Alan Lomax.
Copyright 1936, Folkways Music Publishers, Inc., N.Y. Used by permission.

Three Jolly Fishermen

There were three jol - ly fish - er - men, There were three jol - ly fish - er - men — "Fish - er, fish - er"; "men, men, men." "Fish - er, fish - er"; "men, men, men." There were three jol - ly fish - er - men.

The first one's name was Abraham,
The first one's name was Abraham,
Abra, Abra; ham, ham, ham, etc.

The second one's name was I-I-saac,
The second one's name was I-I-saac,
I-I, I-I; zik, zik, zik, etc.

The third one's name was Ja-a-cob,
The third one's name was Ja-a-cob,
Ja-a, Ja-a; cub, cub, cub, etc.

They all went up to Jericho,
They all went up to Jericho,

Jer-i, Jer-i; cho, cho, cho, etc.

They should have gone to Amsterdam,
They should have gone to Amsterdam,
Amster, Amster; sh, sh, sh, etc.

> *Variation: Have one group shout* Fisher, fisher *and a second group shout* men, men, men. *Repeat this for* Abraham, Isaac, Jacob, Jericho, *and* Amsterdam.

Camp Menu Song

To-day is Mon-day! To-day is Mon-day! Mon-day Hasenpfeffer!

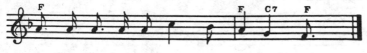

Ev - 'ry- bo - dy hap - py? Well, I should say!

As you sing this song, add a day each time until all days are named.

Today is Tuesday! Tuesday, string beans.
Monday, Hasenpfeffer; everybody happy?
Well, I should say!

Today is Wednesday! Sou-oop, etc.
Today is Thursday! Roast beef, etc.
Today is Friday! Fish, etc.
Today is Saturday! Payday, etc.
Today is Sunday! Church. *Very softly*

> *Variation: Divide into groups; have each group rise and sing one day's menu.*

Throw It Out the Window

Old Moth - er Hub-bard went to the cup-board to

get her poor dog a bone. When she got there the

cup-board was bare, She threw it out the win-dow, the

win-dow, the win-dow, She threw it out the win-dow.

When she got there the cup-board was bare, She

threw it out the win - dow.

Sing as a group song using a new Mother Goose rhyme each time you repeat melody. Substitute She threw it out the window *for last line of each rhyme and make throwing motions with arms.*

24

Mary had a little lamb,
Its fleece was white as snow
And everywhere that Mary went
She threw it out the window,
The window, the window,
She threw it out the window.
And everywhere that Mary went
She threw it out the window.

Variation: Divide the group into two or more teams. One team starts by singing a rhyme. As soon as one team finishes, another starts. A team is eliminated if it fails to start singing as soon as its turn comes.

O Chester!

Tune: "Yankee Doodle"

Sing through once without action. Repeat four times, acting out an additional line each time.

O Chester, did you 'ear about Harry?
   Strike chest, touch ears, pat head.
He "chest" got back from the Army.
   Strike chest and back, then fold arms.
I 'ear he knows how to wear a rose,
   Touch ear, nose, lapel.
Hip! Hip! Hooray — for the Army!
   Raise fists for cheers; fold arms.

Ham and Eggs

Tune: "Tammany"

Ham and eggs, Ham and eggs,

I like mine fried nice and brown.

I like mine fried up side down.

Ham and eggs, Ham and eggs,

Flip'em Flop'em Flop'em Flip'em Ham and eggs!

Variation: Divide boys into two groups and sing a second time. Tap knees rapidly to imitate frying.

Ham and eggs,
   First group sings.

Ham and eggs,
   Second group sings.

I like mine fried nice and brown.
   First group sings.

26

I like mine fried upside down.
Second group echoes.

Ham and eggs,
First group sings.

Ham and eggs,
Second group yells.

Flip 'em
First group yells.

Flop 'em
Second group yells.

Flop 'em
First group yells.

Flip 'em
Second group yells.

Ham and eggs!
All sing.

Rounds

The Paddle Song

D minor throughout song

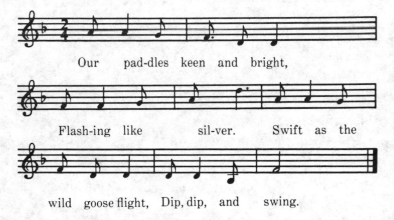

Our pad-dles keen and bright,

Flash-ing like sil-ver. Swift as the

wild goose flight, Dip, dip, and swing.

Some boys can sing throughout song

dip, dip, and swing

Dip, dip, and swing them back,
   Flashing like silver;
Swift as the wild goose flight,
   Dip, dip, and swing.

Hi Ho! Nobody Home

Three-part round

Hi, ho no - bod - y home,

meat nor drink nor mon-ey have I none.

Yet will I be mer - - - r - y.

Three Blind Mice

A round   Key: D.   Time: 6/8

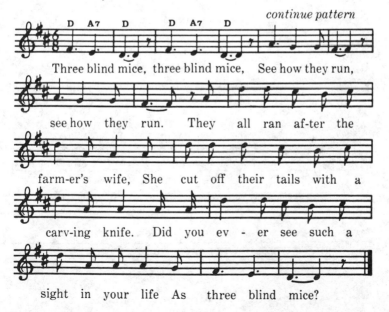

Three blind mice, three blind mice, See how they run,

see how they run. They all ran af-ter the

farm-er's wife, She cut off their tails with a

carv-ing knife. Did you ev - er see such a

sight in your life As three blind mice?

London's Burning

Three-part round

(Continue one chord)

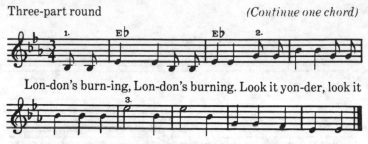

Lon-don's burn-ing, Lon-don's burning. Look it yon-der, look it

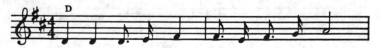

yon-der. Fire, Fire, Fire, Fire, And we have no wa-ter.

Variation: Have part of group (very few) imitate sirens throughout the song, and others may imitate noise of fire equipment by shaking keys, tapping chair or table with pencil, etc.

Row, Row, Row Your Boat

A round

One chord entire song

Row, row, row your boat Gent - ly down the stream;

Mer-ri-ly, mer-ri-ly, mer-ri-ly, mer-ri-ly Life is but a dream.

Down by the Station

Lee Ricks — Slim Gaillard

DOWN BY THE STA - TION ear-ly in the

morn - ing, See the lit-tle puff-er bel-lies

all in a row; See the sta-tion-

mas-ter turn the lit-tle han-dle. Chug, chug,

toot, toot, Off we go.

Are You Sleeping?

A round   Key: F   *One chord entire song*

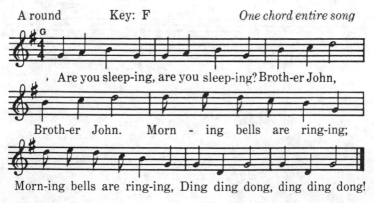

Are you sleep-ing, are you sleep-ing? Broth-er John,

Broth-er John. Morn - ing bells are ring-ing;

Morn-ing bells are ring-ing, Ding ding dong, ding ding dong!

Lively Songs

The Horses Run Around

The hor-ses run a - round, their

feet are on the ground, Oh,

who will wind the clock while I'm a-

way, a- way, Go get the ax, there's a

hair on ba - by's chest; Oh, a

boy's best friend is his mo-ther, his mo-ther.

While looking out the window, a second-story window,
I slipped and sprained my eyebrow on the pavement, the
pavement,

Go get the Listerine, sister has a beau,
Oh, who cut the sleeves off father's vest, his vest.

A-peeking through the knothole, in grandpa's wooden
    leg,
Oh, who has built the shore so near the ocean, the ocean,
Go get the alcohol, Willy wants a rub,
For grandma's teeth will soon fit baby, fit baby.

While walking in the moonlight, the bright and sunny
    moonlight,
She kissed me in the eye with a tomato, tomato,
We feed the baby garlic so we find him in the dark,
An onion, is a husky vegetable, a table.

She spanked him with a shingle, and made his panties
    tingle.
Because he socked his little baby brother, his brother,
A snake's belt always slips, just because he has no hips,
And he wears a necktie around his middle, his middle.

I Want a Girl

Key: C

I want a girl, just like the girl
That married dear old Dad;
She was a pearl and the only girl
That Daddy ever had.
A good, old-fashioned girl with heart so true,
One who loves nobody else but you,
I want a girl, just like the girl
That married dear old Dad.

Ivan Skizavitzsky Skivar

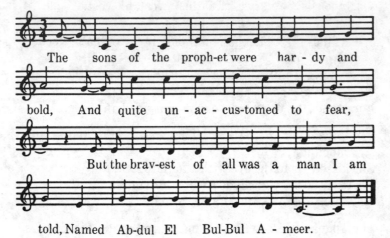

The sons of the proph-et were har-dy and bold, And quite un-ac-cus-tomed to fear, But the brav-est of all was a man I am told, Named Ab-dul El Bul-Bul A - meer.

If they wanted a man to encourage the van,
    Or to harass the foe in the rear;
Or to storm a redoubt, they would set up a shout,
    For Abdul El Bul-Bul Ameer.

There were heroes in plenty and men known to fame,
    Who fought in the ranks of the Czar;
But none of more fame than a man by the name
    Of Ivan Skizavitzsky Skivar.

He could sing like Caruso, both tenor and bass,
    He could play on the Spanish guitar;
In fact, quite the cream of the Muscovite team
    Was Ivan Skizavitzsky Skivar.

One day this bold Muscovite shouldered his gun
    And walked down the street with a sneer;
He was looking for fun when he happened to run
    Upon Abdul El Bul-Bul Ameer.

"Young man," said Bul-Bul, "is existence so dull,
    That you're anxious to end your career?

For, infidel, know you have trod on the toe
    Of Abdul El Bul-Bul Ameer.

"So take your last look at the sunshine and brook,
    And send your regrets to the Czar;
By which I imply that you are going to die,
    Mister Ivan Skizavitzsky Skivar."

I've Been Workin' on the Railroad

I've been workin' on the railroad
All the livelong day,
I've been workin' on the railroad
Just to pass the time away;
Can't you hear the whistle blowing?
Rise up so early in the morn;
Can't you hear the captain shouting:
"Dinah blow your horn!"

Dinah won't you blow, Dinah won't you blow,
Dinah won't you blow your horn, your horn!
Dinah won't you blow, Dinah won't you blow,
Dinah won't you blow your horn!

Someone's in the kitchen with Dinah,
Someone's in the kitchen I know;
Someone's in the kitchen with Dinah,
Strummin' on the old banjo.

Fee-fi-fiddely—I—oh!
Fee-fi-fiddely—I—o-o-o-oh!
Fee-fi-fiddely—I—oh!
Strummin' on the old banjo.

Fee-plunk, fi-plunk, fiddely-I-oh plunk!
Fee-fi-fiddely-I-oh, plunk, plunk, plunk!
Fee . . . fi . . . fiddely-I-ohhh . . .
Strummin' on the old banjo.

The Quartermaster's Store

There are mice, mice running through the rice,
At the store, at the store.
There are mice, mice, running through the rice,
At the quartermaster's store.

Repeat chorus.

There are rats, rats, big as alley cats,
At the store, at the store.
There are rats, rats, big as alley cats,
At the quartermaster's store.

Repeat chorus.

John Jacob Jingleheimer Schmidt

John Jac-ob Jin-gle-heim-er Schmidt,

His name is my name too. When-

ev-er we go out, the peo-ple al-ways shout,

"John Jac-ob Jin-gle-heim-er

Schmidt!" Da-da-da-da-da-da-da.

Repeat four times, each time softer until, on the last verse, mouth the first four lines and end by singing Da - da - da - da - da - da - da.

Music used by permission of Rytvoc, Inc., N.Y.

37

The Animal Fair

I went to the an - i - mal fair,— The
birds and the beasts were there.—
The old ba-boon by the light of the moon, Was
comb - ing his au - burn hair.——
The fun - ni - est was the monk,— He
climbed up the el - e - phant's trunk.—
The el - e - phant sneezed and fell on his knees, And
what be - came of the monk? —

The monk, the monk, the monk, the monk.

Variations

When song is sung through once, a small group may sing the

38

last line over and over as a chant while rest sing the song a second time.

Other lyrics for the "monkey" line: "The monkey he got drunk, and fell on the elephant's trunk."

Smile Song

Tune: "John Brown's Body"   Key: B Flat

It isn't any trouble just to S-M-I-L-E,
It isn't any trouble just to S-M-I-L-E.
There isn't any trouble, but will vanish like a bubble,
If you'll only take the trouble just to S-M-I-L-E.

Second verse: It isn't any trouble just to G-R-I-N, Grin, *etc.*
Third verse: It isn't any trouble just to L-A-U-G-H, *etc.*
Fourth verse: It isn't any trouble just to HA! HA! HA!
   HA! HA! *etc.*

Oh! How I Hate To Get Up in the Morning

By Irving Berlin

   Chorus
"Oh! how I hate to get up in the morning,
Oh! how I'd love to remain in bed—
For the hardest blow of all, is to hear the bugler call:
You've got to get up, you've got to get up,
You've got to get up this morning!

Someday I'm going to murder the bugler,
Someday they're going to find him dead—
I'll amputate his reveille, and step upon it heavily,
And spend the rest of my life in bed."

Drool Song

Just plant a wat-er-mel-on seed upon my grave and let the juice run
through. Just plant a watermelon seed up-on my grave, That's
all I ask of you. Chick-en and pos-sum are
might-y fine, But there ain't no taste like a
wat-er-mel-on rind. Just plant a wat-er-mel-on seed upon my grave and let the juice run through.

From *The Scouter*, published by The Boy Scouts Association of Great Britain

Pink Pajamas

Tune: "Battle Hymn of the Republic"

I wear my pink pajamas in the summer when it's hot.
I wear my flannel nighties in the winter when it's not.
And sometimes in the springtime and sometimes in the fall,
I jump right in between the sheets with nothing on at all.

Chorus
Glory, glory, Hallelujah;
Glory, glory, what's it to you.
Balmy breezes blowing through you,
With nothing on at all.

Michael Finnegan

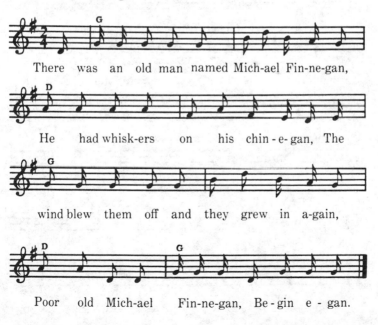

There was an old man named Mich-ael Fin-ne-gan,

He had whisk-ers on his chin - e- gan, The

wind blew them off and they grew in a-gain,

Poor old Mich-ael Fin-ne-gan, Be - gin e - gan.

Patriotic Songs

The Stars and Stripes Forever

Words by Bob Russell

Music by John Philip Sousa

Moderately

There a - loft in a soft and friend - ly

breeze Flies the Red, White, and Blue a - bove

you, And un - furled with her world of

mem - o - ries Of the men who said, who

proud - ly said "I love you."

When I see the Stars and the Stripes, —

— Then my heart is a drum wild - ly beat -

ing, So proud to be part of the dream —

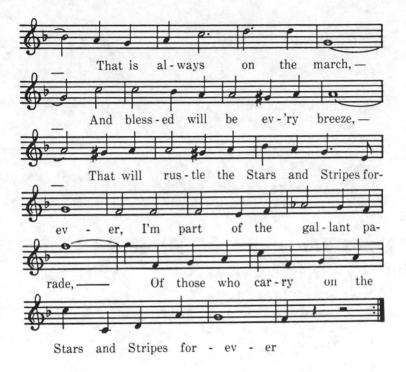

That is al-ways on the march, —

And bless-ed will be ev-'ry breeze, —

That will rus-tle the Stars and Stripes for-

ev - er, I'm part of the gal-lant pa-

rade, —— Of those who car-ry on the

Stars and Stripes for - ev - er

America

By Rev. Samuel F. Smith

Key: G.   Time: 3/4

My country! 'tis of thee,
Sweet land of liberty,
Of thee I sing;
Land where my fathers died,
Land of the pilgrims' pride,
From ev'ry mountain side
Let freedom ring.

My native country, thee,
Land of the noble free,
Thy name I love;
I love thy rocks and rills,
Thy woods and templed hills,
My heart with rapture thrills
Like that above.

Let music swell the breeze,
And ring from all the trees,
Sweet freedom's song;
Let mortal tongues awake,
Let all that breathe partake,
Let rocks their silence break,
The sound prolong.

Our fathers' God, to Thee,
Author of Liberty,
To Thee we sing;
Long may our land be bright
With freedom's holy light,
Protect us by Thy might,
Great God, our King.

God Bless America

By Irving Berlin

Moderately

God bless A - mer - i - ca —— Land that I love —— Stand be - side her —— and guide her — Thru the night with a light from a - bove —— From the moun-tains —— to the prai - ries - — To the o - ceans white with foam — God bless A - mer - i - ca —— My home sweet home —— God bless A - mer-i-ca — — My home sweet home. ——

America, the Beautiful

By Katherine Lee Bates

Key: B Flat.   Time: 4/4

O, beau - ti - ful for spa - cious skies, For
am - ber waves of grain, For pur - ple moun - tain
maj - es - ties A - bove the fruit-ed plain. A -
mer - i - ca! A - mer - i - ca! God
shed His grace on thee, And crown thy good with
broth - er - hood From sea to shin - ing sea.

O, beautiful for pilgrim feet,
Whose stern, impassioned stress,
A thoroughfare for freedom beat,
Across the wilderness!
America! America! God mend thine every flaw,
Confirm thy soul in self-control,
Thy liberty in law!

O, beautiful for heroes proved,
In liberating strife,
Who more than self their country loved,
And mercy more than life!
America! America! May God thy gold refine,
Till all success be nobleness,
And every gain divine!

O, beautiful for patriot dream,
That sees, beyond the years,
Thine alabaster cities gleam,
Undimmed by human tears.
America! America! God shed His Grace on thee,
And crown thy good with brotherhood
From sea to shining sea.

The Star-Spangled Banner

By Francis Scott Key

Key: A Flat.   Time: 3/4

O say, can you see, by the dawn's early light,
What so proudly we hail'd at the twilight's last gleaming?
Whose broad stripes and bright stars, thro' the perilous
    fight,
O'er the ramparts we watched were so gallantly streaming.
And the rockets' red glare, the bombs bursting in air,
Gave proof thro' the night that our flag was still there!
O say, does the star-spangled banner yet wave
O'er the land of the free and the home of the brave?

On the shore, dimly seen thro' the mist of the deep,
Where the foe's haughty host in dread silence reposes,
What is that which the breeze, o'er the towering steep,
As it fitfully blows, half conceals, half discloses?
Now it catches the gleam of the morning's first beam,
In full glory reflected, now shines on the stream—
'Tis the star-spangled banner. O long may it wave
O'er the land of the free and the home of the brave.

Forward America

Music by Larry Corbett, Jr.

For - ward A-mer-i-ca, It's my home and my coun-

try. For - ward A-mer-i-ca, It's the land most

dear to me. We will sing my country 'tis of Thee,

Sweet land of Lib - er - ty As we go For - ward A -

mer - i - ca, It's my home and my coun-try-try.

Songs of Scouting

Boy Scouts of America

Words and music by Jack Combs and Jimmy Clark

We're the Boy Scouts of A-mer-i-ca

Scout-ing for things a - new.

Our ac-tiv-i-ties lead to vic-to-ries in

all we set out to do. We're the Boy

Scouts of A- mer-i- ca, We plan hand in

hand each day To do bet-ter than need be done

till all our goals are won champs with a win-ning way.

We're loy-al   to pur-pose   and in-teg-ri-ty

Pledged to   the Scout Oath e - ter-nal-ly.   With

verve and con- vic-tion   we sing our song   to

keep   A - mer-i - ca strong.   We're the Boy

Scouts of   A - mer- i - ca,   and this we

have to   say   Join us and we'll stand be-

side   you,   be - side   you   all the   way.

The Boy   Scouts   of A - mer-i-   ca

will stand be-side   you   all the way.

There's Something About a Boy Scout

Tune: "There's Something About a Soldier" by Fred Waring

March tempo

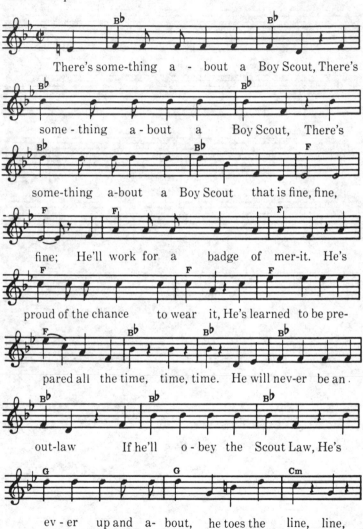

There's some-thing a - bout a Boy Scout, There's some - thing a - bout a Boy Scout, There's some-thing a-bout a Boy Scout that is fine, fine, fine; He'll work for a badge of mer-it. He's proud of the chance to wear it, He's learned to be pre-pared all the time, time, time. He will nev-er be an out-law If he'll o - bey the Scout Law, He's ev - er up and a - bout, he toes the line, line,

line. On his   oath   to   do his   best, That's e-

nough, you know   the rest, There's some-thing a-bout a

Boy Scout that   is   fine,   fine,   fine.

Boom! Boom! Gee It's Great To Be Scouting

Boom!   Boom!   Gee   it's great   to   be

Scout-ing. Boom!   Boom! Gee it's great to be

out-ing, hik-ing   and camp-ing all day long. Boom!

Boom! Gee it's great to   be   Scout - ing!

I've Got That Scouting Spirit

Tune: "Joy in My Heart"

I've got that Scouting spirit,
Up in my head,
Up in my head,
Up in my head.
I've got that Scouting spirit,
Up in my head,
Up in my head, to stay.

I've got that Scouting spirit,
Deep in my heart, etc.
Continue as in first verse.

I've got that Scouting spirit,
Down in my feet, etc.
Continue as in first verse.

I've got that Scouting spirit,
Allover me, etc.
Continue as in first verse.

I've got that Scouting Spirit,
Up in my head,
Deep in my heart,
Down in my feet.
I've got that Scouting spirit,
Allover me,
Allover me, all ways.

Used by permission of John D. Cooke.

Scout Leader's Prayer

Tune: "Marcheta"
By Talman H. Trask

Key: E Flat

Our Fa - ther in Heav - en a-bove us, We
ask Thee for guid-ance in our dai - ly task. May
vir-ture and manhood stand strong-ly a-mongst us. To
Thee we give all of our thanks. The
Scout Oath, the Scout Law, their les-sons un-fold-ing To
our youth, in num-bers un - told, Our
mot-to, our Good Turn, may we live it and teach it, Great
Spir - it of Scout - ing we pray.

Be Prepared

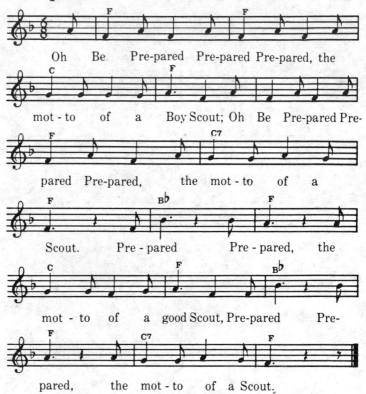

Oh Be Pre-pared Pre-pared Pre-pared, the mot - to of a Boy Scout; Oh Be Pre-pared Pre-pared Pre-pared, the mot - to of a Scout. Pre - pared Pre - pared, the mot - to of a good Scout, Pre-pared Pre-pared, the mot - to of a Scout.

We're on the Upward Trail

We're on the upward trail,
We're on the upward trail,
Singing as we go. Scouting bound.
We're on the upward trail,
We're on the upward trail,
Singing, singing, ev'rybody singing,
Scouting bound.

Hiking

Tune: "Caisson Song"

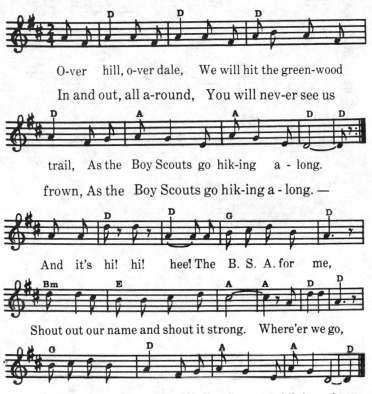

O-ver hill, o-ver dale, We will hit the green-wood

In and out, all a-round, You will nev-er see us

trail, As the Boy Scouts go hik-ing a - long.

frown, As the Boy Scouts go hik-ing a - long. —

And it's hi! hi! hee! The B. S. A. for me,

Shout out our name and shout it strong. Where'er we go,

we will al-ways know That the Boy Scouts go hik-ing a-long.

Philmont Grace

For food, for raiment,
For life, for opportunity,
For friendship and fellowship . . .
We thank Thee, O Lord.

Philmont Hymn

Sil - ver on the sage, Star - lit skies a-bove,

As - pen cov-ered hills, Coun - try that I love,

Phil-mont here's to thee, Scout - ing par - a - dise,

Out in God's coun-try to - night.

Wind in whis-p'ring pines, Ea - gle soar-ing high,

Pur - ple moun-tains rise, A-gainst an a-zure sky,

Phil-mont here's to thee, Scout-ing par-a-dise,

Out in God's coun - try to - night.

Trail the Eagle

Tune: "On Wisconsin"   Key: C.   Time: 2/4

Trail the Eagle,
Trail the Eagle,
Climbing all the time.
First the Star and then the Life,
Will on your bosom shine.

Keep climbing!
Blaze the trail and we will follow,
Hark the Eagle's call;
On, brothers, on until we're Eagles all.

Pack Up Your Troubles

Tune: "Smile, Smile, Smile"
By George Asaf

Pack up your troubles in your old kit-bag,
And smile, smile, smile.

Now we're a'hiking on the old Scout trail,
Smile, boys, that's the style.

What's the use of worrying?
It never was worthwhile ... SOOO!

Pack up your troubles in your old kit-bag,
And smile, smile, smile.

The Torch of Scouting

Words by O.A. Kirkham

Music by V.E. Carroll

For - ward ye sons of men who with might and main, Worked to pre-serve and build a Na - tion. Now with cour - age true, we will dare and do. Know - ing that right is ev - er with us. Car - ry high the torch ev - er mar-ching. Car - ry high the torch of true Scout - ing. For-ward ye sons might and main. We will pre-serve and build a Na-tion.

Scout's Good-Night Song

Tune: "Santa Lucia"

Foot-steps on dis-tant trail Camp-ward are bend-ing;

Birch fire and bub-bling stew Rich o-dors send-ing;

Here is your heart's de-sire, Rest when your feet shall tire;

O - pen air and pals and food and fire; Joy nev'er end-ing.

Campfires are burning low,
  No longer leaping;
Scouts sing their evening song,
  Shadows come creeping;
Sun sinks below the west,
  Good-night and may you rest;
Blankets warm and by soft sounds caressed;
  Scouts all are sleeping.

61

A Boy Scout's Prayer

Words and music by Gwen Beck

Now the day is done; Boy Scouts one by one,

Bow your head in prayer to the Lord up there.

Oh I thank you for this beau-ti-ful day, Oh Lord.

Thank you for the moun-tains, the trees in the lane;

Thank you for the sun-shine that shines through the rain;

Thank you for this beau-ti-ful day. And as I

camp on the trail to-night, and I raise my

eyes to the moon-lit sky, and I pray, Oh

hear my prayers to-night. Lord I thank you for this

beau - ti - ful day.　　A - - men.

On My Honor

Words and music by Harry Bartelt

On my hon - or I'll do my best to do my
du - ty to God. On my hon - or I'll do my
best to serve my coun-try as I may. On my
hon-or I'll do my best to do my Good Turn each
day To keep my bod-y strength-ened and
keep my mind a - wakened. To fol-low paths of
right-eous-ness. On my hon - or I'll do my best.

Camporee or Jamboree Hymn

Words and music by M.H. McMasters

Blaz - ing camp-fires make our spir - its light,

As we meet in fel - low - ship to - night;

Scouts u - nit - ed for a world that's free,

Fires have light - ed in our jam-bo-ree.

Fading campfires 'neath a starry sky,
   Silv'ry bugles sound their lullaby,
Scouting friendships fashioned here today,
   Bind us closer—when we are away.

Father, guide us, where brave men have trod,
   Help us know the Fatherhood of God,
Here beside us—let us know Thy plan,
   May we show the Brotherhood of Man.

I'm Happy When I'm Hiking

English hiking song

Tramp, tramp, tramp, tramp, tramp, tramp, tramp, tramp.

I'm hap - py when I'm hik - ing, pack up - on my

back.   I'm hap - py when I'm hik - ing   off the beat - en

track.   Out in the o - pen   coun-try, that's the place for

me.   With a true Scout-ing friend   to the jour-ney's end,

ten, twen-ty, thir - ty,   for - ty,   fif - ty   miles   a

day.   Tramp, tramp, tramp.   *(Repeat tramp to end.)*

Scouting Marches On

O.B. Mathews   John T. Boudreau

Scout-ing march-es, Scout-ing march-es, Scout-ing march - es on.—— Strong and read - y, true and stead-y, Till the goal is won. —— Daunt-ed nev-er, cour-age ev-er, For the right FIGHT ON! —— To our home-land ev - er loy - al Scout - ing march - es on.——

Scouting We Go

Hail! Hail! Scouting Spirit

Tune: "My Hero"—from *The Chocolate Soldier*

Key: B Flat

Hail! Hail! Scouting Spirit,
   Best in the land;
Hail! Hail! Scouting Spirit,
   Loyal we stand.
Onward and upward we're treading,
   Always alert to make Scouting ready,
We are prepared.
Hail! Hail! Scouting Spirit.
Hail! Hail! Hail!

You Can Tell a Scout

Tune: "Long, Long Trail"
Key: A Flat.   Time: 4/4

You can tell a Scout from . . .
Insert troop number, city, or camp name in place of dotted lines.

You can tell him by his talk;
You can tell a Scout from . . .
You can tell him by his walk;
You can tell him by his manner,
By his appetite and such.
You can tell a Scout from . . .
But you cannot tell him much.

Scout Hearted Men

Tune: "Stout Hearted Men"

Give me some men, who are Scout hearted men,
    Who will fight for the right they adore.

Start me with ten, who are Scout hearted men,
    And I'll soon give you ten thousand more.

Oh! Shoulder to shoulder and bolder and bolder
    They grow as they go on the fore!

Then — There's nothing in the world can halt or mar a plan
When Scout hearted men can stick together man to man!

Here's to the Boy Scouts

Here's to the Boy Scouts of A - mer - i - ca! Here's to the

Scouts where-ev-er they may be, A sal-ute to ev-'ry Scout we

meet, Not a one shall know de - feat. Be - e Pre-

pared our mot-to ev-er be. Our em-blem is the fleur-de-

lis. Our Oath and Law we will o - bey, And we'll

a Good Turn ev - 'ry day!

Western Ballads

Back in the Saddle Again

Words and music by Gene Autry and Ray Whitley

I'm back in the sad - dle a - gain ——

Out where a friend is a friend —— Where the

long-horn cat - tle feed, on the low - ly jim - son

weed; I'm back in the sad - dle a - gain. —— Rid-in' the

range once more, Tot - in' my old fort - y - four ——

Where you sleep out ev-'ry - night where the   on-ly law is right;   I'm back   in   the   sad - dle   a - gain. —

Whoo - pi -   ti - yi -   yo   Rock-in' to and fro back   in   the   sad   dle   a-   gain. ——

Whoo   - pi - ti - yi - ya   I   go   my   way ——

back   in   the   sad - dle   a -   gain. ——

The Old Chisolm Trail

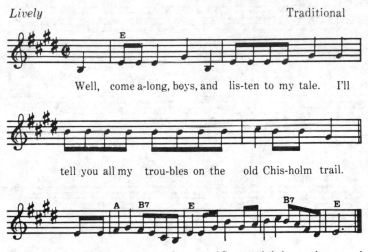

Lively   Traditional

Well, come a-long, boys, and lis-ten to my tale. I'll

tell you all my trou-bles on the old Chis-holm trail.

Come-a ti yi yi yip-py, yip-py yay, yip-py yay! Come-a ti yi yi yip-py, yip-py yay!

On a ten dollar horse and a forty dollar saddle
I started out a-punchin' those long-horned cattle.

I'm up in the morning before daylight
And before I gets to sleepin' the old moon's shining bright.

Oh, it's bacon and beans almost every single day
And I'd sooner be a-eatin' prairie hay.

I went to the boss for to draw my roll,
He had it figured out I was nine dollars in the hole.

So I went up to the boss and said I won't take that
And I slapped him in the face with my old slouch hat.

I'll sell my outfit just as soon as I can,
'Cause I ain't punchin' cattle for no mean boss man.

With my knees in the saddle and my seat in the sky,
I'll quit punchin' cattle in the sweet by and by.

Red River Valley

Not too slow

From this val - ley they say you are go - ing, We will miss your bright eyes and sweet smile, For they say you are tak - ing the sun - shine,——— That ——— bright - ens our path - way a - while.

Refrain

Come and sit by my side if you love me,— Do not hast - en to bid me a - dieu,— But re- mem- ber the Red Riv - er Val - ley, And the girl that has loved you so true.—

Continued on next page

Do you think of the valley you're leaving?
Oh, how lonely, how sad it will be.
Oh, think of the fond heart you're breaking,
And the grief you are causing me to see.

From this valley they say you are going;
When you go, may your darling go, too?
Would you leave her behind unprotected,
When she loves no other but you?

As you go to your home by the ocean,
May you never forget those sweet hours that we spent
    in the Red River Valley,
And the love we exchanged 'mid the flow'rs.

The Cowboy's Sweet Bye and Bye

Tune: "My Bonnie"

Key: G.   Time: 3/4

Last night as I lay on the prairie
And gazed at the stars in the skies,
I wondered if ever a cowboy
Could drift to that sweet bye and bye.

Chorus
Roll on, roll on,
Roll on, little dogies,
Roll on, roll on,
Roll on, roll on,
Roll on little dogies, roll on.

The road to that bright heavenly region
Is a dim narrow trail, so they say,
But the road that leads down to perdition
Is posted and blazed all the way.

Repeat chorus.

They speak of another Great Owner
Who's never o'erstocked, so they say
But who always makes room for the sinner
Who drifts from the straight narrow way.

Repeat chorus.

74

They tell of another great roundup,
Where cowboys like dogies will stand,
To be marked by the Riders of Judgment,
Who are posted and know every brand.

Repeat chorus.

Courtesy of Bill Pollock.

Home on the Range

Oh give me a home where the buf-fa-lo roam, Where the
deer and the an-te-lope play. Where sel-dom is heard a dis-
cour-ag-ing word, And the skies are not cloud-y all day.
Home, home on the range, Where the deer and the an-te-lope
play— Where sel-dom is heard a dis-
cour-ag-ing word, And the skies are not cloud-y all day.

Where the air is so pure,
The zephyrs so free,
The breezes so balmy and lite,
That I would not exchange my home on the range,
For all of the cities so brite

Clementine

Key: G. Time: 3/4

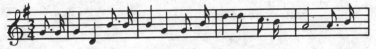

In a cav-ern, in a can-yon, Ex-ca-vat-ing for a mine, Dwelt a

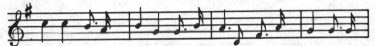

min-er, For-ty-nin-er, And his daugh-ter, Cle-men-tine. Oh my

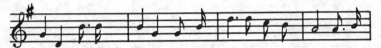

dar-ling, Oh my dar-ling, Oh my dar-ling Cle-men-tine, You are

lost and gone for-ev-er, Dread-ful sor-ry, Cle-men-tine.

Chorus

Light she was and like a fairy,
   And her shoes were number nine;
Herring boxes, without topses,
   Sandals were for Clementine.

   Repeat chorus.

Drove she ducklings to the water,
   Ev'ry morning just at nine;
Hit her foot against a splinter,
   Fell into the foaming brine.

   Repeat chorus.

Saw her lips above the water,
  Blowing bubbles, mighty fine;
But alas! I was no swimmer,
  So I lost my Clementine.

  Repeat chorus.

Old Paint

Smoothly   Cowboy song

Good - by,   old Paint, I'm a-leav-ing Chey - enne,

My foot in the stir - rup, my po - ny won't stand;

I'm a - leav-ing   Chey-enne and I'm off to Mon - tan'.

Good - by,   old Paint, I'm a - leav - ing Chey - enne.

I'm riding old Paint and a leading old Fan;
Good-by, little Annie, I'm off to Montan'.
Good-by, old Paint, I'm a-leaving Cheyenne.
Go hitch up your horses and give them some hay,
And seat yourself by me as long as you stay.
Good-by, old Paint, I'm a-leaving Cheyenne.

The Dying Cowboy

Rather slowly

"O bur- y me not on the lone prairie"; These words came low and mourn-ful-
ly, From the pal- lid lips of a youth who
lay On his dy - ing
bed at the close of day.

It matters not, I've oft been told,

Where the body lies when the heart grows cold,

Yet grant, oh grant this wish to me:

O bury me not on the lone prairie.

"O bury me not" and his voice failed there,

But we took no heed of his dying prayer.

In a narrow grave just six by three,

We buried him there on the lone prairie.

And the cowboys now as they roam the plain,

For they marked the spot where his bones were lain,

Fling a handful of roses o'er his grave,

With a prayer to Him who his soul will save.

The Happy Wanderer

Antonia Ridge   Friedn W. Möller

I love to go a-wander-ing, A-long the
moun-tain track,—And as I go, I love to
sing, My knap-sack on my back.—Val-de
ri— Val-de ra— Val-de ra— Val-de
ha ha ha ha ha ha Val-de ri,— Val-de
ra. My knap-sack on my back.

I love to wander by the stream
    That dances in the sun,
So joyously it calls to me,
    "Come! Join my happy song!"

I wave my hat to all I meet,
    And they wave back to me,
And blackbirds call so loud and sweet
    From ev'ry green-wood tree.

High overhead, the skylarks wing,
    They never rest at home
But just like me, they love to sing,
    As o'er the world we roam.

Oh, may I go awandering
    Until the day I die!
Oh, may I always laugh and sing,
    Beneath God's clear blue sky!

By special permission of the Sam Fox Publishing Company, Inc.

This Land Is Your Land

Woody Guthrie   Gospel Tune

This land is your land,—this land is my land,—
From Cal-i-for-nia—to the New York Is-land,
From the red-wood for-est—to the Gulf Stream wa-ters,
This land was made for you and me.——

As I went walking that ribbon of highway
I saw above me that endless skyway,
I saw below me that golden valley,
This land was made for you and me.

I roamed and rambled, and I followed my footsteps,
To the sparkling sands of her diamond deserts,
All around me a voice was sounding,
This land was made for you and me.

When the sun came shining, than I was strolling,
And the wheat fields waving, and the dust clouds rolling,
A voice was chanting as the fog was lifting,
This land was made for you and me.

Chaparral Song

In the land of the Las - sen, where

tim - ber is tall, There are cer - tain brush

patch - es through which we must crawl Some

spe - cies are lim - ber, while oth - ers are

stiff; And they all will fly

back at your nose with a biff.

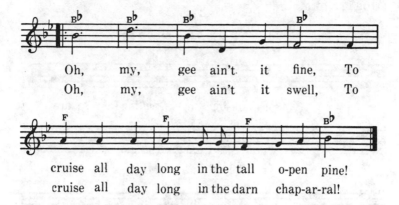

Oh, my, gee ain't it fine, To
Oh, my, gee ain't it swell, To

cruise all day long in the tall o-pen pine!
cruise all day long in the darn chap-ar-ral!

Oh, we might ride the saddle of a ridge we could stick;
We might spear our grub with the fork of a crick;
Use the riverbed to sleep on;
Eat sawdust for mush,
But we can't scrub our teeth with this darn hillside brush.

Chorus

Dogie Song

Sung rhythmically to the swing of riding a horse

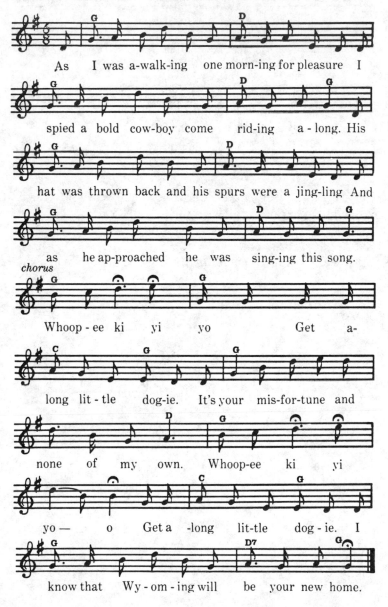

As I was a-walk-ing one morn-ing for pleasure I spied a bold cow-boy come rid-ing a - long. His hat was thrown back and his spurs were a jing-ling And as he ap-proached he was sing-ing this song.

chorus

Whoop - ee ki yi yo Get a- long lit - tle dog-ie. It's your mis-for-tune and none of my own. Whoop-ee ki yi yo — o Get a -long lit-tle dog - ie. I know that Wy - om - ing will be your new home.

84

It's early in the springtime, we round up the dogies,
  Mark—and brand—and bob off their tails;
Round up the ponies—load up the chuck wagon,
  And throw the dogies out onto the trail.

chorus

Shenandoah

Slowly   Traditional

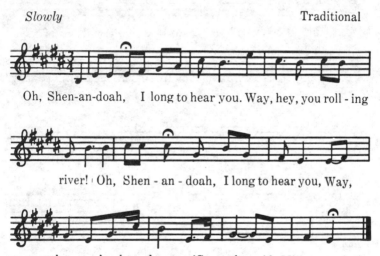

Oh, Shen-an-doah,   I long to hear you. Way, hey, you roll - ing

river! Oh, Shen - an - doah, I long to hear you, Way,

hey, we ' re bound a-way 'Cross the wide Mis - sour - i.

Oh, Shenandoah, I love your daughter,
Way, hey, you rolling river!
Oh, Shenandoah, I love your daughter,
Way, hey, we're bound away 'cross the wide Missouri.

Oh, Shenandoah, I'm bound to leave you,
Way, hey, you rolling river!
Oh, Shenandoah, I'll not deceive you,
Way, hey, we're bound away 'cross the wide Missouri.

International Songs

Waltzing Matilda

Once a jol-ly swag-man

camped by a bil-la-bong Un-der the shade of a

cool-i-bah tree, And he sang as he watched and

wait-ed till his bil-ly boiled,

"You'll come a-waltz-ing, Ma-til-da, with me!"

chorus.

Waltz-ing Ma-til-da, waltz-ing Ma-til-da,

You'll come a-waltz-ing Ma-til-da with me. And he

sang as he watched and wait-ed till his bil-ly boiled.

"You'll come a-waltz-ing   Ma-til-da with me!"

Down came a jumbuck to drink beside the billabong,

    Up jumped the swagman and seized him with glee;

And he sang as he talked to that jumbuck in his tucker-bag;*

    "You'll come a-waltzing, Matilda, with me."
Repeat chorus.

Down came the stockman, riding on his thoroughbred;

    Down came the troopers one, two, three.

"Where's the jolly jumbuck, you've got in your tucker-bag?*

"You'll come a-waltzing, Matilda, with me."
Repeat chorus.

Up jumped the swagman and plunged into the billabong,

    "You'll never catch me alive," cried he.

And his ghost may be heard as you ride beside the billa-bong,*

"You'll come a-waltzing, Matilda, with me."
Repeat chorus.

Substitute this line for third line of chorus

Used by permission of Carl Fischer, Inc., N.Y.

Walking at Night

Translated version and
Czech folk song by A.D. Zanzig

Walk-ing at night a - long the mead - ow way,

Home from the dance be - side my maid - en gay,

Walk - ing at night a - long the mead - ow way,

Home from the dance be - side my maid - en gay. Hey!

Much faster *but second time* pp

Sto - do - le, sto - do - le, sto - do - le, pum - pa,

Sto - do - le, pum - pa, sto - do - le, pum - pa,

Sto - do - le, sto - do - le, sto - do - le, pum - pa,

Sto - do - le, pum - pa, pum, pum, pum.

Nearing the wood, we heard the nightingale,
Sweetly it echoed over hill and dale.
Nearing the wood, we heard the nightingale,
Sweetly it echoed over hill and dale. Hey!

Many the stars that brightly shone above,
But none so bright as her one word of love.
Many the stars that brightly shone above,
But none so bright as her one word of love. Hey!

From *Singing America*, published by C. C. Birchard and Co., Boston. Used by permission of publisher and National Recreation Assn., copyright owner.

Auld Lang Syne

By Robert Burns

Should auld acquaintance be forgot,
And never bro't to mind?
Should auld acquaintance be forgot
And days of auld lang syne?

Chorus
For auld lang syne, my dear,
For auld lang syne;
We'll tak' a cup o' kindness yet
For auld lang syne.

And here's a hand, my trusty friend,
And gie's a hand o' thine;
We'll tak' a cup o' kindness yet,
For auld lang syne.

Repeat chorus.

Zum Gali Gali

Palestinian Folk Tune
Key: E minor

Steadily

As we work we sing a song, We sing it all day long.
When we reach the end of the day, We will dance, and sing, and be gay.

Zum ga-li ga-li gal-li, Zum gal-li gal-li, Zum ga-li gal-li gal-li, Zum ga-li gal-li.

Alouette

French-Canadian canoe song

Allegretto

Each time you sing the melody, add a new word in the measure before the Oh! *Have group repeat this and sing all preceding verses in reverse.*

3. Le nez; 4. Le cou; 5. Le pied; 6. Le dos; 7. Les pattes

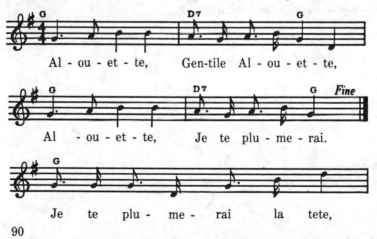

Al - ou - et - te,   Gen-tile Al - ou - et - te,

Al - ou - et - te,   Je te plu - me - rai.

Je te plu - me - rai   la tete,

90

Je te plu - me - rai la tete.

chorus.

Et la tete; Et la tete; Oh!

The Far Northland

Tune: "Road to the Isles"—from *Songs of the Hebrides*
By M. Kennedy-Fraser

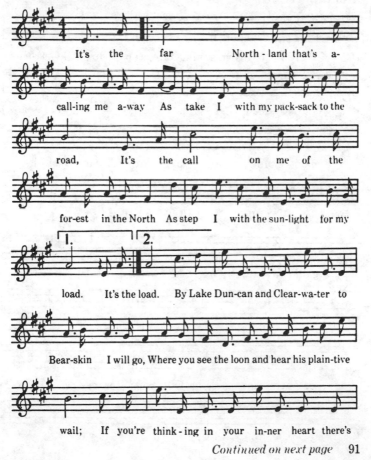

It's the far North - land that's a-

call-ing me a-way As take I with my pack-sack to the

road, It's the call on me of the

for-est in the North As step I with the sun-light for my

1. **2.**

load. It's the load. By Lake Dun-can and Clear-wa-ter to

Bear-skin I will go, Where you see the loon and hear his plain-tive

wail; If you're think - ing in your in - ner heart there's

Continued on next page 91

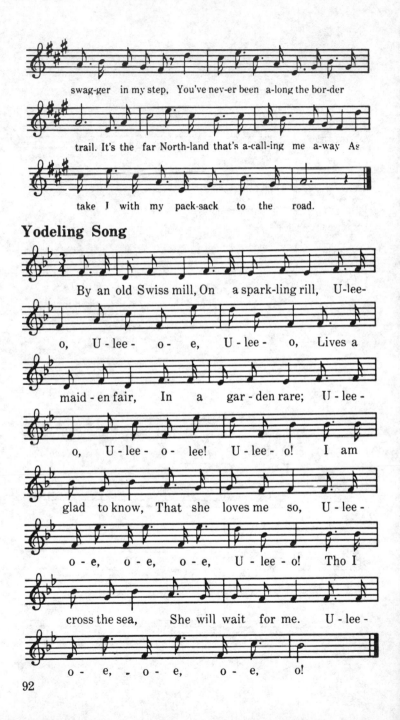

swag-ger in my step, You've nev-er been a-long the bor-der

trail. It's the far North-land that's a-call-ing me a-way As

take I with my pack-sack to the road.

Yodeling Song

By an old Swiss mill, On a spark-ling rill, U-lee-

o, U-lee - o - e, U-lee - o, Lives a

maid - en fair, In a gar - den rare; U - lee -

o, U - lee - o - lee! U - lee - o! I am

glad to know, That she loves me so, U - lee -

o - e, o - e, o - e, U - lee - o! Tho I

cross the sea, She will wait for me. U - lee -

o - e, - o - e, o - e, o!

The Herdsman

With spirit

1. The — herds - man — is — mer - ry, he —— sings all day long; He — seek - eth — his — flock — as he —— chant - eth this song. Ho - le - a, Ho - le - e - e - e - a, Ho - lé - a, Ho-le-é - é - é - a. Ho - lé - a, Ho-le-é- é - é - a, Ho - lé - a, Ho - le-é-é-a!

In the morning he is milking on the hillside till noon,
But at evening Bellé calls him:
"Come Hans!" "Coming soon."

Folk Songs and Spirituals

Battle Hymn of the Republic

Folk melody   Key: B Flat. Time: 4/4
By Julia Ward Howe

Mine eyes have seen the glory of the coming of the Lord;
He is trampling out the vintage where the grapes of wrath
  are stored;
He hath loosed the fateful lightning of His terrible swift
  sword;
His truth is marching on.

> *Chorus*
> Glory, glory! Hallelujah!
> Glory, glory! Hallelujah!
> Glory, glory! Hallelujah!
> His truth is marching on.

I have seen Him in the watchfires of a hundred circling
  camps;
They have builded Him an altar in the evening dews and
  damps;
I can read His righteous sentence by the dim and flaring
  lamps;
His day is marching on.

> *Repeat chorus.*

He has sounded forth the trumpet that shall never call
  retreat;
He is sifting out the hearts of men before His judgment
  seat;
Oh, be swift, my soul, to answer Him! be jubilant, my
  feet!
Our God is marching on.

> *Repeat chorus.*

Roll, Jordan, Roll

Roll, Jor-dan, roll, Roll, Jor-dan, roll. I
want to go to Heav-en when I die, to hear Jor-dan roll.
1. Oh, broth-ers, you ought t'have been there, Yes, my
Lord! A - sit-ting in the Kingdom, To hear Jor-dan roll.

Oh, preachers, you ought t'have been there,
Yes, my Lord! A-sitting in the Kingdom,
To hear Jordan roll.

Michael Row the Boat Ashore

Mich - ael, row the boat a- shore, Hal - le -
lu - jah! Mich - ael, row the boat a -
shore, Hal - le - lu — jah!

You Can Dig My Grave

You can dig my grave with a sil-ver spade, You can dig my grave with a sil-ver spade, You can dig my grave with a sil-ver spade, Cause I ain't a-gon-na be here much long-er.

There's a long white robe up in Heaven for me,
There's a long white robe up in Heaven for me,
There's a long white robe up in Heaven for me,
'Cause I ain't a-gonna be here much longer.

There's a starry crown up in Heaven for me,
There's a starry crown up in Heaven for me,
There's a starry crown up in Heaven for me,
'Cause I ain't a-gonna be here much longer.

There's a golden harp up in Heaven for me,
There's a golden harp up in Heaven for me,
There's a golden harp up in Heaven for me,
'Cause I ain't a-gonna be here much longer.

You can pluck one string and the whole Heaven rings,
You can pluck one string and the whole Heaven rings,
You can pluck one string and the whole Heaven rings,
'Cause I ain't a-gonna be here much longer.

Repeat first verse.

Jacob's Ladder

Key: B Flat

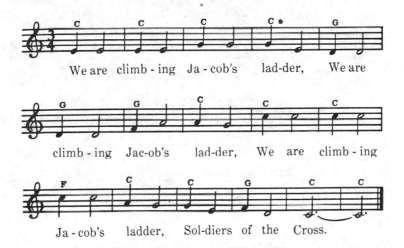

We are climb-ing Ja-cob's lad-der, We are climb-ing Jac-ob's lad-der, We are climb-ing Ja-cob's ladder, Sol-diers of the Cross.

Every round goes higher and higher, etc.
Soldiers of the cross.

Do you think I'd make a soldier? etc.
Soldiers of the cross.

Yes, I'd like to be a soldier, etc.
Soldiers of the cross.

We are climbing higher and higher, etc.
Soldiers of the cross.

In the Good Old Summertime

In the good old sum-mer-time,

In the good old sum-mer-time,

Stroll-ing thro' the sha - dy lanes,

With your ba - by mine; You

hold her hand and she holds yours, And

that's a ve - ry good sign That

she's your toot - sey woot - sey in the

good old sum - mer - time.

Down in the Valley

Down in the val - ley, the val-ley so low,

Hang your head o - ver, hear the wind blow;

Hear the wind blow, dear, hear the wind blow;

Hang your head o - ver, hear the wind blow.

Write me a letter containing three lines,
Answer my question: Will you be mine?
Will you be mine, dear? Will you be mine?
Answer my question: Will you be mine?

Build me a castle forty feet high,
So I can see her, as she rides by;
As she rides by, dear, as she rides by;
So I can see her, as she rides by.

Roses love sunshine, violets love dew,
Angels in heaven, know I love you;
Know I love you, dear, know I love you;
Angels in heaven, know I love you.

Green Grow the Rushes, Oh

Leader *All*

I'll sing you one Ho. Green grow the rush-es, oh,

Leader

what is your one Ho! One is one and all a-lone and

Leader

ev - er more shall be-e so. I'll sing you two Hos.

All

Green grow the rush - es, oh, what are your two Hos!

Leader

Two two the lil - y white boys clothed and all in green ho.

All

One is one and all a-lone and ev-er more shall be-e so.

Leader *All*

I'll sing you three Hos. Green grow the rush-es, oh,

Leader

what are your three Hos. Three three the ri - vals.

All

Two two the lil-y white boys clothed and all in green ho.

One is one and all a-lone and ev-er more shall be-e so.

Leader continues to add one more verse while group joins in singing back through all of previous verses. This song is a lot of fun and will prove popular with the crowd once they catch on to it.

Four for the gospel makers
Five for the cymbals at your door
Six for the six proud walkers
Seven for the seven stars in the sky
Eight for the April rainers
Nine for the nine bright shiners
Ten for ten commandments
Eleven for the eleven that went to Heaven
Twelve for the twelve apostles

Dixie

Words and music by Dan D. Emmett
Key: C

I wish I was in the land of cotton,
Old times there are not forgotten;
Look away! Look away! Look away! Dixieland.
In Dixieland where I was born in,
Early on one frosty mornin';
Look away! Look away! Look away! Dixieland.

Chorus
Then I wish I was in Dixie, Hooray! Hooray!
In Dixieland I'll take my stand to live and die in Dixie;
Away, away, away down south in Dixie.
Away, away, away down south in Dixie.

There's buckwheat cakes and Indian batter,
Makes you fat or a little fatter;
Look away! Look away! Look away! Dixieland.
Then hoe it down and scratch your grabble,
To Dixieland I'm bound to travel,
Look away! Look away! Look away! Dixieland.

Repeat chorus.

He's Got the Whole World in His Hands

Moderately fast

He's got the whole world

in His hands, He's got the big, roun' world

in His hands, He's got the wide world

in His hands; He's got the whole world in His hands.

He's got the wind and the rain in His hands,
He's got the sun and the moon in His hands,
He's got the wind and the rain in His hands;
He's got the whole world in His hands.

He's got the little bitty baby in His hands,
He's got the little bitty baby in His hands,
He's got the little bitty baby in His hands;
He's got the whole world in His hands.

He's got you and me, brother, in His hands,
He's got you and me, brother, in His hands,
He's got you and me, brother, in His hands;
He's got the whole world in His hands.

He's got everybody here in His hands,
He's got everybody here in His hands,
He's got everybody here in His hands;
He's got the whole world in His hands.

He's got the whole world in His hands,
He's got the whole wide world in His hands,
He's got the whole world in His hands;
He's got the whole world in His hands.

I Got Shoes

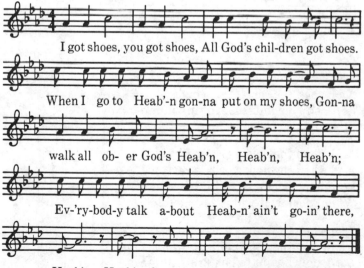

I got shoes, you got shoes, All God's chil-dren got shoes.

When I go to Heab'-n gon-na put on my shoes, Gon-na

walk all ob- er God's Heab'n, Heab'n, Heab'n;

Ev-'ry-bod-y talk a-bout Heab-n' ain't go-in' there,

Heab'n, Heab'n, Gon-na walk all ob-er God's Heab'n.

When the Saints Go Marching In

Oh, when the Saints go march-ing
in, Oh, when the Saints go
march - ing in, Lord, I want to
be in that num-ber, When the
Saints go march - ing in.

And when the revelation comes,
And when the revelation comes,
Lord, how I want to be in that number,
When the revelation comes.

And when the new world is revealed,
And when the new world is revealed,
Lord, how I want to be in that number,
When the new world is revealed.

And when the sun begins to shine,
And when the sun begins to shine,
Lord, how I want to be in that number,
When the sun begins to shine.

104

And when they gather 'round the throne,
And when they gather 'round the throne,
Lord, how I want to be in that number,
When they gather 'round the throne.

Blow the Man Down

Oh, blow the man down, lad-dies, blow the man down,

Way, aye, blow the man down! Oh, blow the man

down, lad-dies, blow the man down,

Give us some time to blow the man down.

Swing Low, Sweet Chariot

chorus Swing low, sweet char - i - ot,

Com - in' for to cary - ry me home,

Swing low, sweet char - i - ot,

Fine

Com - in' for to car - ry me home.

I	looked	o-ver	Jor-dan	and	what did	I	see,
If	you	get	there	be -	fore	I	do,
The	bright-est	day	that	ev-er	I	saw,
I'm	some - times	up	and	some -	times	down,

Com-in' for to car - ry me home,

A
Tell
When
But

band	of	an - gels	com-in'	af-ter	me,
all	my friends	I'm	com -	in'	too,
Heav -	en wash'd	my	sins	a -	way,
still	my	soul	feels	heav'n - ly	bound,

Com - in'   for   to   car - ry   me home.

Oh, Susanna

By Stephen Foster

Key: F

I come from Alabama,
With my banjo on my knee;
I'm going to Louisiana,
My true love for to see.
It rained all night the day I left,
The weather it was dry;
The sun so hot I froze to death;
Susanna, don't you cry.

Chorus
Oh, Susanna, oh, don't you cry for me;
I've come from Alabama,
With my banjo on my knee.
Oh, Susanna, oh, don't you cry for me;
I've come from Alabama.
With my banjo on my knee.

I had a dream the other night,
When everything was still;
I thought I saw Susanna
A-coming down the hill.
The buckwheat cake was in her mouth,
The tear was in her eye;
Says I, I'm coming from the South;
Susanna, don't you cry.

Repeat chorus.

Kum Ba Yah

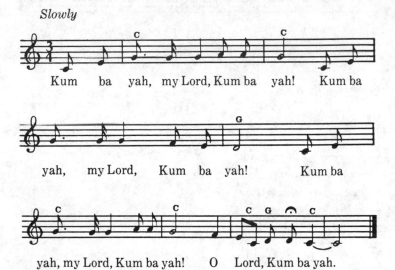

Slowly

Kum   ba   yah,   my Lord,   Kum ba   yah!   Kum ba

yah,   my Lord,   Kum   ba   yah!   Kum ba

yah, my Lord, Kum ba yah!   O   Lord, Kum ba yah.

Someone's crying, Lord, Kum ba yah!
Someone's crying, Lord, Kum ba yah!
Someone's crying, Lord, Kum ba yah!
O Lord, Kum ba ya.

Someone's singing, Lord, Kum ba yah!
Someone's singing, Lord, Kum ba yah!
Someone's singing, Lord, Kum ba yah!
O Lord, Kum ba ya.

Someone's praying, Lord, Kum ba yah!
Someone's praying, Lord, Kum ba yah!
Someone's praying, Lord, Kum ba yah!
O Lord, Kum ba ya.

SCOUT LAW VERSION

(Repeat verse with score.)

A Scout is trustworthy, Lord, Kum ba yah!
A Scout is loyal, Lord, Kum ba yah!
A Scout is helpful, Lord, Kum ba yah!
O Lord, Kum ba ya.

A Scout is friendly, Lord, Kum ba yah!
A Scout is courteous, Lord, Kum ba yah!
A Scout is kind, Lord, Kum ba yah!
O Lord, Kum ba ya.

A Scout is obedient, Lord, Kum ba yah!
A Scout is cheerful, Lord, Kum ba yah!
A Scout is thrifty, Lord, Kum ba yah!
O Lord, Kum ba ya.

A Scout is brave, Lord, Kum ba yah!
A Scout is clean, Lord, Kum ba yah!
A Scout is reverent, Lord, Kum ba yah!
O Lord, Kum ba ya.

These words were introduced at the National Council Annual Meeting held in Cleveland, Ohio, May 1964.

Songs of Inspiration

Onward, Christian Soldiers

Key: E Flat
By Sabine Baring-Gould and Sir Arthur Seymour Sullivan

Onward, Christian soldiers!
Marching as to war,
With the cross of Jesus
Going on before.
Christ, the royal Master,
Leads against the foe;
Forward into battle,
See His banners go!

Chorus
Onward, Christian soldiers,
Marching as to war,
With the cross of Jesus
Going on before.

Onward, then, ye people,
Join our happy throng,
Blend with ours your voices
In the triumph song;
Glory, laud, and honor
Unto Christ the King;
This thro' countless ages
Men and angels sing.

Repeat chorus.

Grace

By Marie Gaudettel

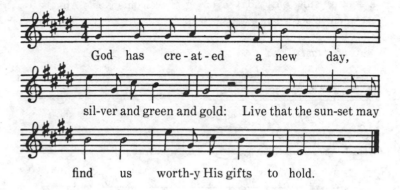

God has cre - at - ed a new day,

sil-ver and green and gold: Live that the sun-set may

find us worth-y His gifts to hold.

Grace Song

By Gen. Lew Wallace and Laurence Danforth

"Fath-er of all God:— What we have

here is of Thee; Take Thou our

thanks and bless us, Help us to do Thy will."

Sholom A'leychem

Peace to You, Angels of God. Give Us of Your Blessings.
A melody sung on Friday evening to welcome God's Angels to
the home in accordance with legend   I. Goldfarb

Not too fast

Sho-lom a'-ley-chem mal-a'-chey ha-sho-reys

mal-a'-chey el - yon Mi -me-lech

ma-chey ha-m' lo-chim ha-ko-dosh bo-ruch hu.

Bo-a'-chem l'- sho-lom mal-a'-chey ha-sho-lom

mal - a' - chey el - yon Mi - me - lech

mal-chey ha- - m' lo-chim ha-ko-dosh bu - ruch hu.

Bor-chu- ni l'-sho- lom mal-a'-chey ha-sho-lom

mal-a'-chey el - yon Mi - me-lech

mal-chey ha - m'lo-chim ha-ko-dosh bo - ruch hu.

Come, O Sabbath Day

A simple melody in keeping with the Sabbath, the day of rest
By G. Gottheil and A.W. Binder

Slowly

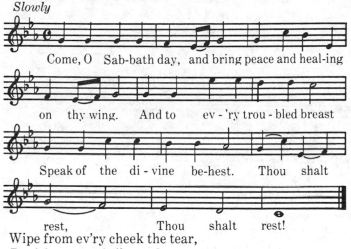

Come, O Sab-bath day, and bring peace and heal-ing
on thy wing. And to ev-'ry trou-bled breast
Speak of the di-vine be-hest. Thou shalt
rest, Thou shalt rest!

Wipe from ev'ry cheek the tear,
Banish care and silence fear.
All things working for the best,
Teach us the divine behest.
Thou shalt rest, Thou shalt rest!

O Come, All Ye Faithful

Tune: "*Adeste Fideles*"
Key: A

O come, all ye faithful, joyful and triumphant,
O come ye, O come ye to Bethlehem!
Come and behold Him, born the King of Angels!

O come, let us adore Him,
O come, let us adore Him,
O come, let us adore Him, Christ, the Lord.

Abide With Me

Henry F. Lyte, 1847   William H. Monk, 1861

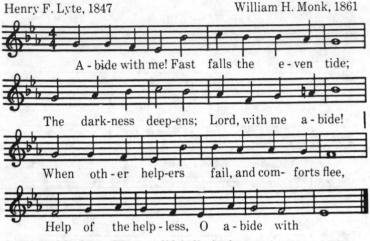

A - bide with me! Fast falls the e - ven tide;

The dark-ness deep-ens; Lord, with me a - bide!

When oth - er help-ers fail, and com- forts flee,

Help of the help - less, O a - bide with

Swift to its close ebbs out life's little day;
Earth's joys grow dim, its glories pass away;
Change and decay in all around I see;
O Thou who changest not, abide with me!

Faith of Our Fathers

Key: G

Faith of our fathers, living still,
In spite of dungeon, fire, and sword;
O how our hearts beat high with joy,
Whene'er we hear that glorious word.

Chorus
Faith of our fathers, holy faith,
We will be true to thee till death.

Faith of our fathers, we will strive,
To win all nations unto thee;
And through the truth that comes from God,
Mankind shall then indeed be free.
Repeat chorus.

Father, We Thank Thee for the Night

By Rebecca J. Weston and Daniel Batchellor

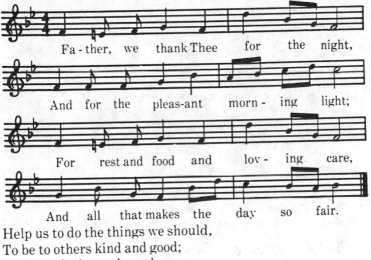

Fa-ther, we thank Thee for the night,
And for the pleas-ant morn-ing light;
For rest and food and lov-ing care,
And all that makes the day so fair.

Help us to do the things we should,
To be to others kind and good;
In all we do, in work or play,
To grow more loving ev'ry day.

O Worship the King

Key: A Flat

O worship the King all glorious above,
O gratefully sing His power and His love;
Our Shield and Defender, the Ancient of Days,
Pavilioned in splendor, and girded with praise.

The earth, with its store of wonders untold,
Almighty, Thy power hath founded of old,
Hath stablished it fast by a changeless decree,
And round it hath cast, like a mantle, the sea.

Thy bountiful care what tongue can recite?
It breathes in the air, it shines in the light,
It steams from the hills, it descends to the plain,
And sweetly distills in the dew and the rain.

All Hail the Power of Jesus' Name

Tune: "Coronation"
By Edward Perronet and Oliver Holden

All hail the power of Jesus' name!
Let angels prostrate fall;
Bring forth the royal diadem,
And crown Him Lord of all.   *(Repeat last two lines)*

Crown Him, ye morning stars of light,
Who fixed this floating ball;
Now hail the strength of Israel's might,
And crown Him Lord of all.   *(Repeat last two lines)*

Let ev'ry kindred, ev'ry tribe
On this terrestrial ball
To Him all majesty ascribe,
And crown Him Lord of all.   *(Repeat last two lines)*

Oh, that with yonder sacred throng
We at His feet may fall;
We'll join the everlasting song,
And crown Him Lord of all.   *(Repeat last two lines)*

Work for the Night Is Coming

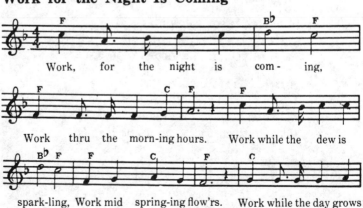

Work, for the night is com-ing,
Work thru the morn-ing hours. Work while the dew is
spark-ling, Work mid spring-ing flow'rs. Work while the day grows

bright - er Un - der the glow-ing sun.

Work, for the night is com-ing, When man's work is done.

Work, for the night is coming,
Work thru the sunny noon.
Fill brightest hours with labor,
Rest comes sure and soon.

Give ev'ry flying minute
Something to keep in store.
Work, for the night is coming,
When man's work is o'er.

Church in the Wildwood

There's a church in the valley by the wildwood,
No lovelier place in the dale,
No spot is so dear to my childhood,
As the little brown church in the vale.

Chorus
O, come, come, come, come,
Come to the church in the wildwood,
O, come to the church in the dale,
No spot is so dear to my childhood,
As the little brown church in the vale.

How sweet on a bright Sabbath morning,
To list to the clear ringing bell,
Its tones so sweetly are calling,
O, come to the church in the vale.

Repeat chorus.

117

Day Is Dying in the West

Tune: "Chautauqua"
Key: A Flat.   Time: 6/4

Day is dying in the west,
Heaven is touching earth with rest;
Wait and worship while the night
Sets her evening lamps a-light
Through all the sky.

   Chorus
Holy, holy, holy, Lord God of hosts!
Heaven and earth are full of Thee,
Heaven and earth are praising Thee,
O Lord Most High!

When forever from our sight,
Pass the stars, the day, the night,
Lord of angels, on our eyes
Let eternal morning rise,
And shadows end.

   Repeat chorus.

Come, Thou Almighty King

Key: G

Come, Thou Almighty King,
Help us Thy name to sing,
Help us to praise:
Father! all-glorious,
O'er all victorious,
Come and reign over us,
Ancient of Days!

118

Come, holy Comforter!
Thy sacred witness bear
In this glad hour:
Thou, who almighty art,
Now rule in every heart,
And ne'er from us depart,
Spirit of power!

My Father's House

Oh, won't you come with me to my fath-er's house, To my fath-er's house, to my Fath-er's house. Oh, won't you come with me to my Fath-er's house. There is peace, peace, peace.

There's sweet communion there, in my Father's house,
In my Father's house, in my Father's house.
There's sweet communion there, in my Father's house.
There is peace, peace, peace.

There'll be no parting there, in my Father's house,
In my Father's house, in my Father's house.
There'll be no parting there, in my Father's house.
There is peace, peace, peace.

A'don Olom

Lord of the World, Who Reigned Alone While Yet the Universe Was Naught, With Him My Soul Rests in Fearless Calm.

The traditional Jewish hymn which ends the Sabbath and high holyday services

Moderately

A' - don o - lom   a' - sher mo - lach   B' -

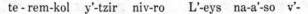

te - rem-kol y'-tzir niv-ro   L'-eys na-a'-so v'-

chef-tzo kol A - zay   me-lech sh'-mo nik-ro.

V'ach-aray kich-los ha-kole
L-vah-do yim-loch no-raw
V'hoo haw-yah, v'hoo ho-veh
V'hoo yee-yeh b'sif-araw.

B'yah-do af-kid roo-chee
B'ace e-shan v'ah-eraw
V'im roo-chee g'vee-yah-see
Adonoi lee v'lo e-raw.

Campfire Ballads

There's a Long, Long Trail

Key: G

There's a long, long trail a-winding
Into the land of my dreams,
Where the nightingales are singing
And a white moon beams:

There's a long, long night of waiting
Until my dreams all come true;
Till the day when I'll be going down
That long, long trail with you.

Used by permission of M. Witmark & Sons, N.Y., copyright owners.

Around the Campfire Bright

O.A. Kirkham

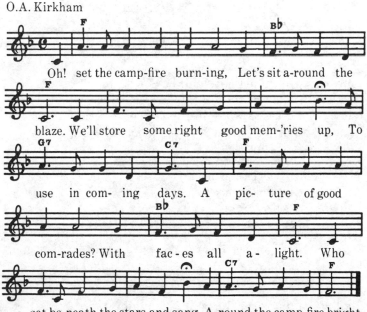

Oh! set the camp-fire burn-ing, Let's sit a-round the
blaze. We'll store some right good mem-'ries up, To
use in com- ing days. A pic- ture of good
com-rades? With fac - es all a - light. Who
sat be-neath the stars and sang, A-round the camp-fire bright.

121

Tell Me Why

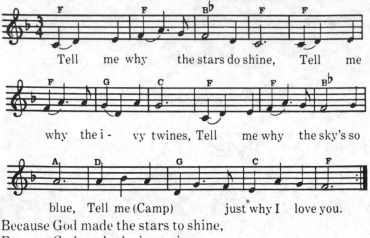

Tell me why the stars do shine, Tell me
why the i - vy twines, Tell me why the sky's so
blue, Tell me (Camp) just why I love you.

Because God made the stars to shine,
Because God made the ivy twine,
Because God made the skies so blue,
Dear old (Camp) . that's why I love you.

Campfire Medley

Key: G

Our boys will shine tonite, our boys will shine;
Our boys will shine tonite, all down the line.
They're all dressed up tonite, don't they look fine!
When the sun goes down, and the moon comes up,
Our boys will shine.

My Bonnie lies over the ocean,
My Bonnie lies over the sea;
My Bonnie lies over the ocean,
O, bring back my Bonnie to me.

Bring back, bring back, O bring back my Bonnie to me,
    to me;
Bring back, bring back, O bring back my Bonnie to me.

Sailing, sailing, over the bounding main,

For many a stormy wind shall blow
Ere Jack comes home again!

Repeat.

Key: F

Goodnight, ladies! Goodnight, ladies!
Goodnight, ladies! We're going to leave you now.
Merrily we roll along, roll along, roll along,
Merrily we roll along, o'er the deep blue sea.

In the Evening by the Moonlight

James A. Bland   *Not too slow*

In the ev-'ning by the moon-light You could
hear those camp-ers sing-ing, In the
ev-'ning by the moon-light You could
hear those ech-oes ring-ing. How the
camp-ers would en-joy it! They would
sit all night and lis-ten As we
sang in the ev'-ning by the moon-light.

Vive l'Amour

A friend on your left, and a friend on your right,
Vive la compagnie!
In love and good fellowship let us unite,
Vive la compagnie!

Repeat chorus.

Now wider and wider our circle expands,
Vive la compagnie!
We sing to our comrades in faraway lands,
Vive la compagnie!

Repeat chorus.

Scout Vesper

Tune: "Tannenbaum"
Key: G.   Time: 3/4

Softly falls the light of day,
While our campfire fades away.
Silently each Scout should ask:
"Have I done my daily task?
Have I kept my honor bright?
Can I guiltless sleep tonight?
Have I done and have I dared
Everything to be prepared?"

By the Blazing Council Fire

Tune: "Till We Meet Again"
Key: A Flat.   Time: 3/4

By the blazing council fire's light,
We have met in comradeship tonight.
Round about the whispering trees
Guard our golden memories
And so before we close our eyes in sleep,
Let us pledge each other that we'll keep
Scouting friendships, strong and deep,
Till me meet again.

Song title used by permission of Remick Music Corp., copyright owner.

Taps

Key: F.   Time: 4/4

Day is done, gone the sun,
From the lake, from the hills,
From the sky;
All is well, safely rest,
God is nigh.

Fading light dims the sight,
And a star gems the sky,
Gleaming bright,
From afar, drawing nigh,
Falls the night.

Index